THE
POWER
WITHIN

THE POWER WITHIN

INTERNAL COMMUNICATIONS,
AN EXECUTIVE'S EDGE IN BUSINESS STRATEGY

MICHELLE S. MORRIS AND TORIN M. LEE

Library of Congress Control Number: 2012903905
ISBN: Hardcover   978-1-4691-7749-6
                  Softcover   978-1-4691-7748-9
                  Ebook   978-1-4691-7750-2

This book was printed in the United States of America.

To order additional copies of this book, contact:
Xlibris Corporation
1-888-795-4274
www.Xlibris.com
Orders@Xlibris.com
109912

CONTENTS

Chapter 1
What Are We Talking About? 7

Chapter 2
It's about Results 8

Chapter 3
Tactics Versus Strategy 10

Chapter 4
Access and Partnership (At the Table with the Big Boys and Girls)........12

Chapter 5
Focus and Impact..15

Chapter 6
No Such Thing as a Second-Class Citizen..20

Chapter 7
Knowing Who, Knowing Why, Knowing What...23

Chapter 8
Tag—You're It 26

Chapter 9
The Voice: Technician, Manager, Leader 31

Chapter 10
Leaders at All Levels...34

Chapter 11
Leadership, Not Lingo..38

Chapter 12
The People: Forming the Best Team..42

Chapter 13
Face It—Integration Is the Smartest Move..45

Appendix
Strategy Template 47

Biographies 51

CHAPTER 1

What Are We Talking About?

WHETHER YOU CALL it internal communications, associate communications, employee communications, or employee engagement, the essence of this function all amounts to one thing—the greatest allies or greatest saboteurs of your business or organization.

Finally, after decades of talking *at* the people who work day to day to make our corporations, businesses, and organizations run, employees and the information they receive are being taken more seriously. Gone are the days of cradle-to-grave employment, and gone is the type of employee loyalty that typified most of the twentieth century. And not only gone is the loyalty of the employers to employees, also gone is the brand of employee loyalty that existed until the 1990s.

This points to why we need to view employees as a major stakeholder to be listened to as well as spoken at. To have influence, you must know what those leverage points are and how to use them.

The first thing to recognize is that it is not about *you*; it is about *them*—all those people you know and do not know. The people who have or think they have or will have a stake in what you do or do not do and how you do it. They are the key influencers of your business.

While most modern-day employers usually recognize legislative or regulatory influence or the local planning authority or national media as key influencers, only the most discerning leaders put employees in the same influential category.

Getting the communications with your employees right is a major step and is often challenging. But it is one that is well worth the effort.

CHAPTER 2

It's about Results

NINETY-FIVE PERCENT—MAYBE MORE— of formal communicating people do internally is ineffective, ignored, or saved for a later read—in other words, white noise.

Communicating to check a box on someone's to-do sheet or project plan makes about as much sense as ringing the bell at the stock exchange on a Sunday: no one's there, and no one cares.

If you are a CEO or a senior executive who only wants to use your communications department as an "insurance policy," with people answering the phone to act as a buffer when something goes wrong or putting out an e-mail in times of trouble, or you are a communicator who only wants to check the box and write a report about the number of tasks you completed so people can see how busy you are and then collect a paycheck, then read no further—this book is not for you.

This book is about getting results—business results—through internal communications.

Communications can be one of the most valuable business tools ever. But, it has to be used for that purpose—to advance business goals and objectives.

See if any of the next scenarios sound familiar. They are all cases that were thrown into the lap of a communicator to either make happen or be a part of the team to do it. All examples are very real, and all involved a communications person stepping from the shadows and being the catalyst for success. Some of these have real dollars attached—either in revenue or savings. Some are the heart and soul of the company's very existence. Some changed the perception of what truly effective and efficient communications can do for the bottom line . . .

How important would it be to you if:

- You completely changed your business model and had a five-year plan to increase revenue by 500 percent, but instead you were able to do it in twenty-four months?
- Your business was close to bankruptcy. The SEC was watching every move. You were brought in to turn it around. Unionization efforts were rampant. Yet you were able to measurably get everyone at all levels across the company to understand a new direction, calm down, and work together toward success within six months?
- You had a decentralized organization and could turn it into a high-performing global organization in a year?
- You run a communications department that keeps getting layered but are able to change the way it operates, and now the head of the business wouldn't think of making a move without having you or your team at the table?
- You come in to head an existing staff function. You're in the C-suite, your best and brightest are accustomed to sitting in the background and being the "water carrier" work horses of the business, providing no strategic input or council—and you can turn the function around without firing everyone and starting from scratch?

For the sake of what—why are you communicating? Is it for the sake of your business or organization? If it's because you want to have a real impact and make a real difference for your key stakeholders, read on.

CHAPTER 3

Tactics versus Strategy

A NY COMMUNICATIONS PROFESSIONAL, from a first-year, entry-level employee to the seasoned pro, can put together a list of things *to do*, whether talking about a policy change, layoffs, making an organizational announcement, or the myriad other tasks a communicator is expected to handle.

But how many communications professionals do you know can write a thoughtful, practical communications strategy mapped to a business plan and designed to enable a more effective execution of that business plan? And how many of these communicators actually stick to it?

There are many who think the value of having a communications strategy is negligible because situations continually fluctuate, and communicators need to be able to react.

The difference between those who act without strategy and those who have a living strategy is that those *with* a strategy in position know *how* to react. They know the messages with which to stick or modify rather than create in the moment. They know the impact to the business and what you are striving to achieve together. They do not have to reinvent any wheel. And in general, they are better prepared and can be gracious under fire and confident in the results.

Having a strategy means you are

1. prepared,
2. in line with the business or organizational goals,

3. focused,
4. can measure results, and
5. replicate the effort.

This does not just apply to business. It applies to all sectors and vocations. Strategists are the visionaries that not only lay out where you are going but anticipate the curves in the road. They are able to see a path around when the tree falls because they have the broader full-picture view that provides grounded direction, including alternate paths.

Think of the celebrated tenor. When he sings with an orchestra and a choir, he must follow the conductor, who is the chief strategist of the performance, or the production will be less than optimal. The conductor is the steward of the bigger view and hears not only the single instruments and voices but understands how to make it all fit together in perfect harmony.

The same applies to a communications department without a strategy. Individual tactics can be successful. But the longer-term business benefit can be questionable or suboptimal without an overarching strategy under which all the tactics work together to accomplish something much bigger than individual talent and effort.

CHAPTER 4

Access and Partnership
(At the Table with the Big Boys and Girls)

STRATEGIC COMMUNICATIONS REQUIRES a different level of involvement—and commitment—than which many may be accustomed to.

Communicators need to avoid becoming the short-order cooks—eggs over easy; fries, not hash browns; toast on the side . . . You get the picture. Order takers are one thing; strategic partners are a totally different breed.

To be true business partners, Communications has to have a seat at the table where direction is determined and decisions are made. There is expertise strategic communicators bring to the table that would be completely lost in translation if they are only informed of the short orders after the fact—things like tone, context, how the pieces fit together, who is truly on board, and who is hovering. Communicators have a highly trained intuitive side. Observation is key to a lot of what we do: the words *not* used, the words used, the body language. All complete the total picture and color the counsel the senior executive gets outside the room.

As one communicator said to a potential employer, "If you are looking for a 'yes' person, I am not that person. What you will have from me is complete loyalty to you and your business and always counsel what's in the best interest of you, your customers, and employees. But if you want me to do that and help you find your voice, articulate where you're taking the business, and sound like you, I have to be in the room where the decisions are made . . . I need to be your shadow." He took the challenge, she got the job, and he ended up being revered internally and externally as a great communicator and true leader.

If the communicator positions herself or himself appropriately, that seat at the table becomes Switzerland—the neutral party that takes all input into account and comes out with the articulation of the best path for the business. Trust and discretion are imperative for the communicator to be successful.

Positioned correctly and holding to a higher standard, the communicator becomes the wartime consigliere to the head of the business, the peacetime confidante, and the enthusiastic catalyst in times of growth, and, at all times, the thought partner and a steward of the company's conscience and soul. It can be the most intimate and tenuous of roles at the same time. This requires a person who is not interested in power for himself/herself but motivated by doing what is right for the business or organization. This may be why very few people actually fulfill this role, and fewer yet do it well.

Once there was a wise, well-respected head of a division of a large Fortune 100 company. This leader had been the architect of a key reorganization. Now this new unit needed to quickly become a functioning, cohesive internal service partner to the rest of the multinational corporation. He said, "I know we need to improve our communications with our employees to make this integration a success. But there is resistance from all sides. The management consultants have already been here, but still we haven't been able to move the needle in some areas of our new business strategy."

The communicator responded, "That's what I do. I not only help you tell employees what you think they need to know, but I also will ask your employees what you and the leaders of this division need to know. The tactics will come easily once we know what we have through this intelligence. The only way to know this is to *ask* your employees." Thus, the executive agreed to give the communicator access to employees at all levels of the organization, and her "asking" began. Through various face-to-face and phone interviews as well as team discussions across all areas of the division, the communicator then could draft a strategy that was sure to address the gaps and tipping points.

In addition, it is this initial research process that enables the communicator to prove his or her loyalty (to leadership, managers, and all employees), mediation abilities, and strategic value to leadership and to the entire organization by helping resolve business issues—*and* holding sacred what individuals divulged. By the time the strategy began to be implemented, the communicator was thought of as a trusted confidant by change agents across the division and had earned that coveted seat at the table.

Getting a seat at the table is sometimes determined before someone takes the lead or executive communications role, as in a previous example: "In order for me to take this job and be successful, I have to be in the room where decisions are made."

Sometimes, it's being in the company for a while and level setting with the business head—"Here is how much more value I can add if I have a seat at the table or at least a chair in the same room."

Chemistry probably has a lot to do with it more than anything else. Some people simply get along better with certain other people—it's not an experience thing or a skills thing (usually), but it is a chemistry, gut-intuition thing.

Whatever the ultimate rationale is, Communications cannot play a strategic role without access to the head of the business and senior team. By the same token, Communications cannot play a strategic role if they do not spend time throughout the organization, experiencing the culture at all levels and actively listening to the people.

The right person positioned effectively can help drive business results—it's almost like magic.

MICHELLE S. MORRIS AND TORIN M. LEE

CHAPTER 5

Focus and Impact

APPROACHING INTERNAL COMMUNICATIONS as a strategic investment is a different way of being. And with different ways of being, there should be a new beginning.

The beginning here is doing the appropriate due diligence—research—up front so you are no longer throwing spaghetti against the wall to see what sticks. You are able to be targeted and far more effective and efficient, which saves time and energy, and even money.

The up-front research/due diligence necessary to target communications and get the biggest bang for your buck is the very marrow of strategic communications. It provides what you need to know and have to have to get out of the spaghetti-throwing business.

Focus on that which you really want to have an impact with the communications.

Speed is critical in today's business world and taking the time to understand your employees up front will get you there faster in the end.

As a communicator, you have to have the fortitude to stand up and push for what you know is right and will be able to measure in the end. As a senior executive, you should expect this level of targeting as a prudent business decision.

Yes, most people want to get to the "doing" and check things off the list—write the organizational announcement, prepare the town hall, etc. But taking the time to clarify with some precision—to understand the topography before planting the trees, so to speak—will determine the right approach to get your people to understand, buy in, and even change behavior, if necessary.

Once a business head cajoled and coerced a communications manager to come work for him with tales of desperate need and shared glory. When there, he said, "Great, you're here. I need a newsletter." She said, "No." He said, "But I want one." She said, "Okay, you can have your newsletter *if* you pay for perception research to be done before I write your communications plan and *if* I can design the newsletter." He said, "Deal."

And so it went. He got more than he bargained for with the communications professional and with his newsletter. She explained to him how newsletters were passive forms of communications that check a box so people are lulled into thinking everyone in the organization is now "informed." What they really become is a "nice to read . . . if I have time . . . stay in the pile" mode of communication. If it can wait for a newsletter (printed or online), then it probably is not urgent, and no action need be taken. Checking the box really does not translate into having an impact, and an impact is what you need if you truly want to align people behind your direction.

In the case of this business executive who was completely changing his business and needed alignment across the organization, the newsletter became this cool, funky, visually appealing piece with lots of white space, original art, and short, context-rich stories that provided the foundation for his vision and a platform for his ideas. Everyone around the world got to read the same thing at the same time, in their own language, with no interpretation and manipulation from the middle.

But let's get back to the other part of the deal—the research. There are many types of research and many different companies that conduct it. However, a particularly effective methodology is perception research. The group that perfected this methodology, Decision Partners, LLC, calls it Mental Models Research. It gets at individuals' underlying beliefs and thoughts, ones they might not even personally know they have. The reason this is particularly effective for influencing communications is because it allows you to target. It can be conducted with all the bells and whistles and database support, or guerrilla style—both are highly effective.

MICHELLE S. MORRIS AND TORIN M. LEE

Perception research is not like a survey. Yes, it will tell you what people are thinking at a given point in time. More importantly, it also tells you *why* people think, believe, perceive, and act the way they do. Then it goes even further, and you hear from them what it will take for them to change what they think, believe, perceive, and how they behave. Who wouldn't foam at the mouth to be able to target this closely? Targeting what you do will get to the results faster. It also provides a benchmark, enabling you to measure gaps and see how far you've come over time. In this case, it is clearly a situation of "ask and you shall receive."

In the example of our senior business executive, he only asked if people around the world were behind him in his quest to change the business. This included his senior team, sales, manufacturing, marketing, mail room staff, etc.

What the research was able to show was that none of these people understood what his new vision was for the business, what was driving it, why it was important, what the consequences were for not following him and changing, and what was expected of them. In other words, all they saw was a confusing vision statement that was not at all clear and had no context.

The research was able to pinpoint what each of the groups of people who made up the business needed to see, hear, and understand in order to align behind the head of the business and charge forward with him. They needed information, they needed to be influenced, and they needed to be given clear choices with clear consequences. Even the mail room team needed to know the strategy, and then they could decide what they needed to do to support the new business model.

By targeting the real essence of what needed to be accomplished and what people needed to know and do to get there, a communications strategy was able to have an impact on precisely what the heart of the issue was and help move the business forward more quickly and effectively.

A note of warning is warranted—naked emperors will be very frightened and threatened by perception research. "What? You are going to ask the peasants about ruling the kingdom? For shame!"

A strategic communicator will coax, cajole, and in some cases coerce and stomp his or her feet at the executive to understand and sponsor this highly effective form of research. The bottom line is that it is for a business purpose and will help move the organization forward in a more targeted fashion and more quickly get to the end goal, whatever that may be.

Interviewing individuals one-on-one with open-ended questions that you do not know the answer to before you ask can feel risky to some, but the benefits far outweigh the risks. It also doesn't take a statistically valid number of people to survey. As what Decision Partners will tell you with decades of experience using this methodology, after you've talked to twenty people in a given organization—regardless of what country in which they reside or what age or gender they are, you've heard it all. There are no new categories of thought, ideas, or actions after twenty. Most organizations interview more just to be safe.

The other thing to remember is that not all interviewers are created equal. While anyone or any firm can conduct interviews, how to conduct a true dialogue and what to do with it once you have the data is another story all together. If done internally—what we call guerrilla perception research without all the bell and whistles you get with an outside firm—the interviewers have to be nonthreatening and trustworthy in the eyes of the employees. This rule of thumb generally cuts out senior executives, direct managers or supervisors, and human resources representatives. You will get much richer, unfettered, unvarnished data if you are careful who you pick to conduct the interview and ensure the interviewees remain anonymous.

If we go back to the story of the senior executive who wanted the newsletter, we will find that the perception research yielded surprising results. His own leadership team did not understand where he wanted to go and why. Employees around the world wanted to back him but didn't understand what the business direction was they were supposed to help him achieve. And this new leadership team, with him at the helm, had a very short window of opportunity to act and show results before the honeymoon period was over and people would go back to their own siloed way of thinking and acting. Employees detailed what they needed to hear and see in order to jump on the bandwagon. They specifically outlined what forms of communication worked best for them. The communications strategy that was mapped to the business strategy was targeted, written, and implemented based on the research. There weren't a plethora of exhaustive tactics you might expect would be warranted by this big of an effort. There were *targeted* tactics. The time expected to reach an aligned workforce, in reality, was cut by 60 percent by taking the time up front and getting the lay of the land.

Yes, corporate communications is definitely an art, but it is also sprinkled with science. That science should be used to benefit all. Do all communications professionals worth their salt have a bag of tricks at the ready at any given moment in time? Of course. But why not use communications strategically and cut time, and often expense, by targeting?

CHAPTER 6

No Such Thing as a Second-Class Citizen

INTERNAL COMMUNICATIONS SHOULD feel like a lively conversation among people who trust and respect one another and are working toward a common goal.

Simple. Concise. No ambiguity. No obfuscation (what happened to simple?). Always be direct, because if you are not, trust is lost. Trust is not a negotiation; it's either there, or it isn't. And it is fragile.

In eras past, senior executives would make decisions behind closed doors, and their communications officers would then be expected to relay the outcome to the internal masses. No reasoning. No examination of options. No view into the why or sometimes even the what. Only expected to comply and supply the how. That's the past—a past, remember, where there was loyalty to the company and to its people.

In today's world of instantaneous communication (akin to spontaneous combustion), everyone expects to be able to find what they want or want to know when they want it and how they want it. Moreover, everyone has a voice. Everyone has the ability to comment, build upon, or squash—all at their fingertips. Walking into work does not mean people check their opinions or brains at the door. Very important is to be able to distinguish a "need to know" from the need to express opinions and "be in the know." Providing the information and tools to your people will solve many of the issues for you before they become issues. Giving a voice to all means they have a role in your success or failure.

Not many years ago a head of a fast-growing business in an old-line industry completely changed the business model—including what they were going to sell and to whom they would sell it. The change was unfathomable to most people, from the board of directors to employees in the business—but the leader was making money so was given a lot of leeway. He recognized that the changes meant better articulating what he was trying to accomplish and doing some things completely differently throughout the organization—and without full employee support around the world, he would fail.

The communications manager advised this leader to explain the strategy—to *all* employees. He was advised to start with why the changes had to happen, what was driving them, and then talk about what they needed to do to be a thriving, viable, business. And do it in person in a road show that would span the globe. The leader was worried about "taking it to the people." Others in the business, including other communicators, declared that "regular" employees had no interest, no business, and no capacity to understand such weighty issues as "strategy."

Again, the communications manager advised, cajoled, and pushed the leader—reminding him people didn't check their brains at the security gate. These people ran households, managed budgets, raised children, paid mortgages, were leaders in their churches, synagogues, mosques, and communities. To think business strategy was beyond them was silly. Then the real fear came out. "I don't want to go on this road show of yours and talk about this. They're going to ask me what they need to change or do, and I don't know what to tell someone on the front line to do. I don't have the answer."

The communications manager smiled and reassured the harried leader. "It's okay. Tell them what you're trying to do, why you're doing it—what's driving the change. I guarantee they'll understand and support the change when you flat out say the business will no longer be viable in five years if we don't move into other things because there are too many other companies selling the product we created 25 years ago. They *will* get it. Ask them to help and let *them* tell *you* what it is they are going to do or change to support the move. They're closest to the work—give them some ownership in this; make them part of your vision."

Lo and behold. It worked. People were coming out of the woodwork to help and find better ways to do their jobs and simplify processes. A transition that was scheduled to take five years took twenty-four months. And people had a lot of fun along with the hard work—all along the way.

The activities were a combination of face-to-face meetings, Q&A sessions, talk shows, walk-arounds, and celebrations around the world. This—combined with internal and external speeches and foundational written communications translated into all the appropriate languages—provided an internal window to everything that was happening simultaneously with the external marketing and advertising campaign.

All internal communications stemmed from what was happening, why it was happening, and then the challenge to people to become a part of it. Everything was aimed to enable the employees to make a difference. And they did.

In a modern business or any organization, there is no such thing as a second-class citizen. Everyone has a critical role and shares in the failure or success.

CHAPTER 7

Knowing Who, Knowing Why, Knowing What

ONE OF THE cardinal rules of good communications is knowing what you're trying to accomplish (having objectives in the first place), whom you're trying to influence (yes, influence, not just inform), and what is the most direct path to make it happen (not simply a long laundry list of random activities).

Sounds simple and logical, right? It's amazing how many people, including communicators, don't know what the objectives are and neglect to articulate them. The other common mistake is articulating objectives that the communications team does not directly influence.

For example, stating, "Sales reps will have better relationships with customers, increasing revenue by twenty percent over the previous year," is not within the direct control of the communicator. A better stated objective may be, "Sales reps will have clearly understandable materials at their disposal, a simple and compelling elevator speech, and the necessary communications training in creating a dialogue with customers by the beginning of the sales season, which will help them increase revenue."

Or another example is "Information Technology will complete the upgrade in record time," which is not controlled by the communicator, whereas "Ensure the Information Technology team has clearly stated why the upgrade will require the participation of all managers and provide tools for them to make sure participation is at record levels in record time," is an objective the communicator can directly influence.

Objectives need to be measurable and directly influenced by the communications.

No one wants to fail. Taking the time up front to articulate the need and how communications can and will help will save loads of time and headache down the road.

Define the "who" as finitely as possible. For example, saying a stakeholder is all employees or all shareholders is not terribly helpful, and probably not very accurate. More likely, you'll want to influence a certain segment of your employees or shareholders, or different segments need slightly different methods. Maybe it's the service centers, or the accountants, or major institutional shareholders, or the managers.

Think of the bullseye on a dartboard or the crosshairs in a scope. Narrow your field to best influence those you have to reach or engage to achieve the business objectives. Another aspect is to tier the stakeholders—an example: your first area to target is the managers who need to take specific action, the second tier is the employees they manage who will see and then have an impact on the speed of the action.

Target. Target. Target.

Once you've decided what you're trying to accomplish with the communications and whom you have to involve to meet the business need, find the straightest path to get there.

Every communicator has a bag of tricks and can pull out sheets of paper with lists of random tactics—Web sites, town halls, e-mails, e-cards, teleconference, newsletters (*not* recommended), Webinars, Web conferencing, video tapes, podcasts, speeches, text messages, blogs, Facebook pages, discussion boards, and on and on. Sure, keep throwing enough spaghetti against the wall, and some of it will eventually stick. But this is the major question, how much pasta did you waste in the effort, and how much do you actually have left to eat?

Once a team working on changing the mindset and language of the company to be more customer-friendly wanted to get out its work on words to use and words not to use. The initial thought was to send a copy of the document to the whole company via an e-mail from the president. That quickly devolved in discussions with the communications team.

MICHELLE S. MORRIS AND TORIN M. LEE

In pressing on who really needed to be first in line to change their vocabulary and way of interacting with customers and each other—the inner target on the bullseye—it quickly became apparent that the frontline employees—the call center reps and others who dealt directly with customers each day—were the first and most important target. Service center employees rarely have time to look up nice-to-reads on the intranet or even read the myriad "corporate" e-mails pushed down every day. Doing what they do and having little time for discretionary on-the-job reading, e-mail or an intranet news story was going to be of little use in either informing them or changing their behavior (the ultimate objective). The only way to reach them was up-close-and-personal—their self-espoused preferred communications channel.

In this case, the team took the message on the road in town halls and small group sessions with the people who mattered the most. In a very short period of time, the frontline employees asked senior executives who visited their locations why they were still using the non-customer-friendly language the service centers were leaving behind. Not only did the message get to the people who needed it the most, but it was also fast and effective.

Figure out what will best reach and influence your target stakeholders. Use those methods. It doesn't matter if there are only two tactics in a monthly report if those two tactics effectively and efficiently met the objectives. And keep it real for those you have to influence.

Did we mention you need to target?

CHAPTER 8

Tag—You're It

P RODUCTIVITY, PERFORMANCE, RESULTS. Studies have long shown that a more engaged population is more productive.

The kid who never cleans her room is suddenly motivated by the chance to go to the latest concert (fill in today's hottest teen band) if the room is spotless by dinnertime.

In an organizational environment, people who actively participate in what you're trying to accomplish are more productive, have higher performance, and ultimately deliver results. Come on, it's human nature. One more study is not needed to say it is so.

Just start. You will be surprised, maybe even astounded.

How often these days do you hear (imagine a deep booming voice), "We have to *engage* our employees. We will *empower* them."

Booming voice fades, and a barrage of corporate-speak e-mails assail your inbox . . .

Maybe even a mandatory town hall is held where some big wig in a suit talks at you. In the back of the room, you hear some officious and haggard looking staffer insist that human resources is responsible for employee engagement . . .

Exaggeration? Maybe, but the bet is on that many of you are either smiling or hiding at this point.

Let's get real for a minute. You can't *make* people be engaged. And frankly, HR being solely responsible for employee engagement is ridiculous—they are about policies, governance, compensation, benefits, training, saving money, compliance, employee relations . . . but engagement is not what comes to mind, but for very few exceptions. Engagement—the act of capturing people's attention and getting them to become personally invested and involved in what you are trying to accomplish—is personal. And people, more often than not, have to have a reason to engage. In the corporation, an environment can be created that encourages engagement—as opposed to a stifling, hierarchical, command-and-control culture that does not.

Direct managers are, by far, the most influential in creating space for their people to engage. Even in the most restrictive environments, individual managers have the ability to create the space for creativity and engagement. A manager can also cede some control and power to her people.

But the best world is one where corporations and organizations are enlightened, eagerly embracing the new century way of being. This new way of being is one where people are used to instantaneous news, having choices, being equals, having a voice through social media, and having the right to have a voice in *all* environments. The new generations of young people are open books, whether sharing details on Facebook, Tweeting, or texting incessantly. They expect the same openness in the work environment and are often shocked by what they feel to be the oppressive atmosphere of most corporations.

This new way of being means the culture is open. Leaders set the direction and parameters. The people closest to the work are actually able to act as owners and make decisions about what they do to make it as effective and efficient as possible. The possibilities in this culture are limitless. Empowerment and engagement become a reality—not buzzwords.

If this isn't your culture, something like what we call Tag can help you loosen the creative muscles and give voice to your people. Even if it is your culture, initiatives such as Tag are a great way to up the ante and move to a new level of engagement that leads to and cements alignment with business direction.

"What's Tag?" you may be asking. Remember the children's game—well this is an adult version, which is not a game, but a way to say to one another, "You're it!" Whoever wants to play, plays. Everyone who wants a voice has a voice. This is an effort of the people, by the people, and for the people. Really, it's an executive-free campaign. It's a way for employees to demonstrate their strength, their commitment, and their passion for what they do.

Long before there was Myspace, Facebook, or LinkedIn, there was graffiti. It has been an expression of the masses for decades that ties people together and expresses the sentiments, hopes, dreams, and frustrations of generations. Tag captures the positive aspects of the medium and brings people together in a business setting to achieve the uncommon and untried and do it faster and better. Here we use Tag, the children's game, and tagging—as in graffiti-like activities—to play a game that has serious consequences, if you're willing to play. Consequences that mean you could unleash a huge mass effort of employees acting like owners, having fun, and being engaged to help move your business forward faster and more effectively than ever before.

In this day and age, to move an organization forward, the engagement and alignment of all who work there is imperative. Alignment doesn't happen by edict. It happens on a visceral level by people who believe and have passion for where the leader wants to take them. They talk and act in alignment with his or her agenda.

Bringing that passion out of people and sharing it across an enterprise is powerful, meaningful, and most important, generates positive results.

Rounds of Tag have many different forms. It should start with a leader who says, "Yes, we have to let the voices of the employees be heard and mean something."

Here are some simple examples that have produced powerful results:

- An audio project that captures the voices of individual employees. They discuss the company's direction, what inspires them, what they believe a true leader is and does, and why they keep coming into work each day. Those statements and sentiments are matched with visual depictions that cohere into an "experience" for all to see and hear. There are no executive voices, only the unvarnished thoughts of regular employees.

MICHELLE S. MORRIS AND TORIN M. LEE

- Guerrilla communications that use the words and phrases from employees in sidewalk chalk drawings outside buildings, stickers on floors, static-cling decals on mirrors in bathrooms, dry-erase markers on windows, a Tag wall lined with a tarp/paper where more employees can add their thoughts for all to see, and so much more . . .
- Broken bricks given to employees as mementos and reminders with "Tag—*You* Are It" emblazoned on them.
- Employee-generated videos that depict life and what's going right in their work environment, inspiring others throughout the company.
- An employee film festival, short videos shot and produced "raw" by employees and based on what is important to the company—customer service, community service, business improvement . . . Videos judged, and winners take the red carpet stroll at an awards/film festival viewing event.
- Poster board or flip chart paper in bathrooms, break rooms, and lunch areas posing provocative questions each week and inviting employees to comment.
- Executive blogs with which employees are encouraged to begin a dialogue for all to see.
- Idea discussion boards online where employees can post ideas, add to others' ideas, and have a virtual brainstorm.
- Tagging It Forward—one employee doing something for another, such as a thank you, words of inspiration, writing an inspirational quote on the office window, leaving graffiti-like messages taped to the cubicle wall, and leaving the instructions that "Tag—*you* are it. It's time to Tag It Forward and for you to touch another coworker."
- Employee art exhibits that include the community.
- Volunteering together on a Habitat for Humanity home or the local food pantry and Tag It Forward outside the walls of the company or organization, but do it as a team from the organization.

- What would you add to the list and like to try? Your employees will know what to add once they feel comfortable that the environment will embrace and not punish them for speaking up.

Giving employees choices, allowing them a voice, making them part of the solution, treating them like owners, will reap many rewards in productivity, loyalty, and alignment—all of which will help the business or organization get where it's going faster.

And by the way, it's fun. Let the games begin . . .

MICHELLE S. MORRIS AND TORIN M. LEE

CHAPTER 9

The Voice:
Technician, Manager, Leader

WHEN SOMEONE IS really good at what he or she does, more often than not, the path is to promote that person to manage people.

The only problem with a good theory is this: a good technician does not mean the person will be a good manager. Just as someone who is a really good manager is not necessarily a good leader. It's not ipso facto linear, and it is definitely not a given that one successfully leads to the other.

Technicians can usually be trained to manage. But teaching someone to lead is a whole different proposition and often not a successful one.

Harness your memories for a moment . . .

Who immediately pops into your mind when you think of great *leaders*? More than likely, a statesman, world leader, politician, maybe a great civil rights activist or humanitarian. Rarely does anyone first think of a businessperson as a great leader. Captain of industry, maybe. Titan, maybe. Leader, not usually.

A great technician is the best at whatever her or his discipline is.

A great manager gets the best out of his or her people by leaving them alone to do what they do best, downfield blocking so they don't get overrun by bureaucrats and naysayers, and rolling up the sleeves and helping when asked.

A great leader inspires, sets a direction and course, and creates a culture that allows others to be more and deliver more than they would have imagined on their own. People *want* to follow a great leader.

Good executive communicators help a leader find his or her "voice" and then multiply aligned echoes of that voice by every other executive, manager and, with the right culture, every employee throughout the organization.

"Voice" is more than PowerPoint presentations (actually, it is absolutely *not* PowerPoint presentations). It isn't individual pieces of e-mail to which various and sundry people attach the leader's name. In fact, finding the "voice" is actually harder than most things the leader has to do, including formulating a long-term strategy and short-term delivery plan for the business.

Finding the voice is combining the natural words, rhythm, and cadence of the leader with a consistent message that carries across the entire business and *all* communications. Having something come from the leader that is written by someone else and not in the "voice" is counterproductive, and worse, it is damaging to the credibility of the leader, from whom people have come to expect a certain tone and style.

For example, an annual, pro forma "performance management is coming" e-mail may seem innocuous because it's necessary and an HR policy being reinforced by the leader. But what employees may actually read will sound like corporate-speak and lack credibility, unless highly tailored in the voice of that leader. Often, the "form" message is a time-saving measure that has long-term damaging results to trust and credibility.

A leader's voice resonates with the people when it is and appears to be authentic. Authenticity is rooted in the leader's ownership of the content, the phrasing, and the manner (including tone) in which the message is communicated—regardless of the medium.

Leadership carries an awesome responsibility with it. Good leaders find their voice, lead by example (yes, while words are very powerful, actions

MICHELLE S. MORRIS AND TORIN M. LEE

are what people watch), and inspire others. Good communicators help them to do that in the most effective and powerful way possible. Good communicators are also willing to take a risk and call it out when the word or actions are not befitting the leader.

CHAPTER 10

Leaders at All Levels

"LEADER" IS NOT a title, an income level, or a right. It's not a place on the org chart. It's not the corner office with a great view. While it's often equated with a certain level within a company, the reality is that the moniker "leader" in the pure sense is earned and deserved.

Within a corporation or organization, leaders exist at all levels. One of the biggest internal mistakes made by most organizations is not to harness the power of these individuals.

They are the informal opinion leaders—the ones their coworkers approach when they want a level head or when they want an analysis of the latest unfathomable move by the higher ups. They may technically be an entry-level worker. They may be a great manager everyone clamors to work for and won't leave the organization if they work for that person. It can even be the person in the corner office.

The point is, these are your change agents, your catalysts, your champions, your partners. They are the ones who will make, break, or create a holding pattern. They are the ones you need in order to not only have incremental improvements, but also to harness the energy and commitment of your entire workforce.

Take this example of leadership from the shop floor—literally. In one specialty chemical company, George the welder lived and worked in Wales. He had never managed a team in his life. He was the best welder for hundreds of miles, actually one of the best the company had ever seen. He came to work, did his job, didn't complain, and what the plant managers noticed was that the other workers turned to him for advice and insight not only about welding, but about the company, new policies, leadership changes, even the stock price. George was promoted to supervisor.

George was very nervous about his new position in management and took it very seriously. He made time for the people who reported to him. He mentored them. He asked for training from the company. His business unit decided to try a different type of training that took everyone who managed people, from the president of the business to the frontline supervisor, and put them through the same course—at the same time—promoting the practice of leadership at all levels. George summoned his courage during the course and actually took on the president, critiquing his leadership communications skills, the messages he used, and his actions. He was able to tie it back to what his own team was thinking and seeing. As a result, the president became a better communicator and recognized insight and leadership came from all corners of his business. George gained confidence and was always looking for opportunities for improvement and new ways of doing business that he could pass along.

Another example of leadership at all levels came from part of a Tag initiative implementation. At a utility that had a threat of unionization at one of its largest installations, a new CEO went against the union busters' legal advice. He spent less time talking *at* the frontline workers and instead spent more time listening to them, often staying far longer than his allotted time at the site and not leaving until the last question had been answered or the promise of an answer within seventy-two hours was given.

The CEO and members of his staff took time to find out who the informal opinion leaders were at the site. They spent time talking with them individually and in small groups, listening to them, discussing business and economic realities the company faced, discussing challenges the workers and their families faced. These same informal leaders spent time talking with their colleagues about the CEO and corporate-types who actually listened to them, who actually implemented some of their ideas, who actually understood that the frontline played a huge role in the success of the company. This different style of engagement and recognition of leadership qualities, regardless of hierarchy, spread like a wild fire throughout the company. Other employees listened to these informal opinion leaders and their belief in the sincerity of this new management.

This same method of high-touch employee engagement was replicated across the region, regardless of union or nonunion status. Not only was the threat of unionization in a highly unionized state thwarted, the employee engagement scores across the company were through the roof—an unprecedented ninety-nine percent of employees said they understood the new direction the company was taking, why the changes had to happen, and documented in writing what they needed to personally do to help.

So how do you find these leaders at all levels, these informal opinion leaders?

It's fairly easy—and not all scientific.

Ask—informally. Watch. And listen. You will quickly see who it is that garners the respect of their coworkers.

Then see what they think about things. Bring them in when change is happening and give them a prebrief. Give them the context. Let them know the "why," not just the "what."

And if appropriate, ask for their help. Don't ask them to do anything that would compromise their standing or credibility with their colleagues. Don't penalize them if they decide not to participate in formal programs for you. Just by the fact that they know the context and have a view to the big picture will factor into the words of wisdom they naturally use with their coworkers when asked.

Culture plays a big part in how you can connect the power of these leaders at all levels. In a more open culture, it may happen already. In a toxic or hierarchical culture, it will be more difficult, and you jeopardize the trust and credibility these people naturally engender. Yet it can be accomplished and can all be part of creating a kinder, gentler culture that is open to the alignment and assistance of all "levels" of employees to move your business or organization forward.

Cultivating a culture that encourages leadership at all levels starts with taking the time to listen to employees, what they believe, what they know, their perceptions and perhaps misperceptions. Explain where you are headed and the drivers for that direction. Ask them to help meet your business objectives. When they have ideas, find ways to implement or allow them to implement.

Never "punish" people for having a voice that may differ from yours, instead, spend time persuading and inspiring people with your vision and direction. Highlight ideas that come from anywhere—whether from the mail room, operations unit, or the head of Marketing. Make heroes of every day employees.

Create an informal discussion group that meets with the head of your business to talk about what's happening in the internal and external environment—you can even rotate the people you include. Create content-rich fireside chats where employees from across the organization have the chance to meet with the head of the business in small groups.

Each person you engage with will go back and talk with at least ten others about what you discussed and will carry your message. Soon the effect will be viral and contagious—a really good thing in this day and age.

CHAPTER 11

Leadership, Not Lingo

HAVE YOU DEVELOPED the allergy yet to all things that buzz?

We guarantee your employees have.

Bbbbzzzzzz.

They don't want to "socialize" new ideas or initiatives. (They socialize after work.)

They don't want to be told you are "right-sizing" the company. To them, if you wrong-sized it to begin with, then you and your management team should be the ones penalized. Call it what it is.

They don't want to optimize or utilize. They want to do their best and "use" the tools, skill, and opportunities available to them.

They don't want to hear you're going to "manage the change." Who manages change? You can't do that for them. You need to give them all the information and options, so they can decide if they want to come through the change with you or not. They decide this, not you.

They don't want to be told to think out of the-box or, worse yet, to get in their box.

They don't want to hear about bell curves and performance management programs when they don't get the expected raise or bonus. All workers see through the programs as cost-saving measures that all globally competitive companies need as the competition heats up. They also know performance management can be a way to cover the legal bases when the company chooses to get rid of people.

Hint: What is more compelling and sincere for employees is when you talk about the need for top performance. They understand this. They would rather have managers who do what they are supposed to do and continually manage out marginal workers while rewarding the solid and exceptional people. Most U.S. companies have employment at will anyway—anyone can leave or be let go at any time. This is more difficult outside the United States and subject to local works councils and national laws, but the premise of being straight with employees is the same.

All the corporate-speak, consultant-speak, and latest bbbbuuuuzzzz words in the world are not going to make anyone work harder, understand more, feel the camaraderie, or like you any better. They will, however, give employees the feeling you are masking the truth or, worse yet, hiding something. Throughout history, secret societies have *not* been good for the regular people.

Consider these examples:

- The U.S. chemical company that switched from all employee communications around the world written in English to translations in local languages. This followed from sharing the new vision and strategy with all employees through face-to-face and written communication—strategy had previously been held only at the highest levels. The business was able to shorten their time to goal by 50 percent by engaging and aligning all employees around the world.
- The global technology giant that created a short managers' briefing document in which all corporate-speak, obfuscation, and ambiguity were banned. The document was sent on an as-needed basis as issues arose or announcements were to be made. Managers would get the briefing anywhere from forty-eight hours to one hour before all employees, so they were able to have an intelligent conversation when their teams came to them. Disgruntled managers were reengaged and began accepting their responsibility as managers. The briefing was seen as a sea change for the company culture, and managers consistently cited the briefing during their

training sessions as the most useful management tool they had at the company.

- The tech company that communicated with employees, customers, and distributors only through PowerPoint—and to add insult to injury, the presentations were replete with acronyms that only the most tenured and high-level people in the company could possibly understand. Senior management was very proud of their acronyms. The company was eventually taken over, even though their products were far superior to the competition. While not the deciding factor in their demise, their lack of communications and leadership skills did nothing to help their cause. Instead, they confused distributors, customers, investors, and even their own people.

- The financial services company senior management team went on new-age retreats where they learned a new language that all people in the company eventually picked up, whether they wanted to or not. The consultant spoke with pride about how they were creating a common language to bind the company together and create a sense of belonging . . . Until a new member of the leadership team brought up how there were perfectly good words in English and any other language in the world that should be used. Also mentioned was how some of the usages the consultants had created in their effort to discover the next level of corporate-speak were not even grammatically correct or proper uses of existing words. The clincher was when the new member insisted that creating obscure language was not inclusive, it was actually exclusionary and just downright rude. The language would escape into meetings with customers and business partners, who would scratch their heads and wonder why they were excluded from the secret society. Not surprisingly, the new leader banned the consultant-speak from his team.

Tired of the strident tone of the first paragraphs in this chapter? Good. So are your employees tired of ambiguity, corporate-speak, consultant-speak, and trying to build empty team environments based on a common new language.

MICHELLE S. MORRIS AND TORIN M. LEE

Creating these words or using perfectly good words and giving them a new meaning or grammatical position does not bring people together. It does not build esprit d'corps. Ironically, it is exclusionary. It tells people if they don't know the secret code, they can't join your society. For companies competing in today's world with today's standard of global competition, exclusion should not be on anyone's to-do list.

Inclusive companies and organizations use perfectly good words and speak clearly. They are articulate and intelligent. Sure, some corporate-speak squeezes its way in, but by far, they just tell it like it is. The modern era calls for real leadership, a sense of direction, and common purpose. Words are powerful. Leadership, not lingo.

Develop an allergy to the buzz.

CHAPTER 12

The People:
Forming the Best Team

S O MANY CORPORATIONS spend an inordinate amount of time and energy on how to "develop" their people. This is a nice sentiment. But here is a counter proposal—not opposed, but a parallel path.

If what you are ultimately seeking are business results, it stands to reason you should be picking the people best suited to get results.

Forming a high-functioning, kick-butt communications team is no different.

First, select the strengths you need and then select the people. *After* you've formulated the communications strategy that maps to the business strategy, see where you have strengths and gaps. Figure out what special and foundational skills you need on your team and make it happen.

If you inherited a team, quickly assess people—and not in the traditional way of looking only at their employment record. Talk to them.

- See what they did before they became insiders at your company.
- Ask them what they really like to do.
- Find out what they absolutely hate doing.
- Have them describe something they're really proud of at work.
- Ask them if there's anything else they'd like to be doing other than what they do now.

- If there is something they want to learn, great—find ways for them to get that experience.
- Have them walk you through their work products and then spend time examining the products yourself—communications plans, news releases, publications, reports, etc.

If you have the skills you need, move on to the execution of your plan. If you have gaps, fill them. If you have people that are no longer a good fit for where you're going, quickly help them find another job either internally or externally. Do it all with compassion and grace. And move quickly—don't keep people hanging. It all works out in the end.

If you are building your own communications team from scratch, lucky you. Don't compromise. Determine the skills you need and focus on some you may not automatically think about.

- Diversity is extremely important for a high-performing communications team—and diversity of thought is imperative as well as gender, ethnicity, sexual orientation, and age . . . You have to be able to relate to and communicate with diverse groups of people within your employee base as well as your customer base. Having a diverse team in the first place usually makes that a given in how they operate.
- If you build a team people look at and scratch their heads with puzzled looks on their faces, you're probably on the right track.
- Members of your team may not like one another at the start, but they will learn to respect one another's skills and how they round out the team and play to one another's strengths. One may be an exceptional writer, another a gifted orator, another may be a whiz at social media, or a forward-thinking portal manager, another may be able to put together highly energized business forums, another may be great at project management, one may be an incredibly strategic thinker, while yet another is great with the C-suite, and the person in the next cube is great with the front lines—all are important to where you're trying to take the business.

- Set clear objectives to what you're trying to achieve as a business and let the experts in communications do what they do best—you hired them for their strengths.
- At a minimum, these days, you need strong writers who know how to be simple and concise. You need someone or a team of people who love Web communications and are experts at social media, someone focused on creatively engaging employees, and you need people who can bring a plan to life and execute the tactics.

Basically, the idea is to have and manage a team based on their strengths and potential, not what developmental gaps they have. If they have severe gaps and can't perform what you need them to, then they probably aren't the right people. With entry-level people, of course they need developmental opportunities. You can take a recent liberal arts graduate who can write, think, problem solve, and has the desire, and turn him or her into a fabulous communicator.

Seasoned communications professionals, for the most part, want to know they are valued, do work they like, have someone play to their strengths and recognize them for it, and have fun in a place where they feel they are making a difference. Taking someone who is seasoned and has made a career out of exceptional executive communications and turning to them one day and saying they have a developmental need in Web communications, for instance, is probably going to be nothing but demotivating and insulting.

Have people do what they do best, and you will win with a motivated team. Make sure they share in the limelight and glory, and they will continue to be loyal and motivated. If a head of communication's direct reports and even their direct reports are getting kudos from the business, it only makes the manager and the whole team look better. And as a team, it should be greater together than the sum of the individual parts.

They will produce the necessary business results and put in more than their expected hours—even more than that—to do it. Business leaders will be ecstatic.

MICHELLE S. MORRIS AND TORIN M. LEE

CHAPTER 13

Face It—Integration Is the Smartest Move

PEANUT BUTTER AND jelly. Cereal and milk. Sonny and . . . Cher? Strategy and integration. Let's face it, some things just go together.

While this book is about strategic internal communications, the authors firmly believe the best communications teams are integrated, and the best communications strategies are multipronged and integrated. Period.

In the company, if your primary job is to help influence key stakeholders—in the case of internal communications, it's employees—you should, at the very least, have regular conversations and brainstorm with your colleagues in public relations, government affairs, events management, marketing, and investor relations. In the very best scenario, you will be fully integrated—particularly internal communications, public relations, and executive communications.

A communications strategy that is integrated across internal and external stakeholders has common messaging, a shared objective of influencing all the top stakeholders, and a good view on all the necessary tactics, including how best to use the senior executives' time.

A particularly good structure (it works in both centralized or decentralized teams) is a group of generalist professionals who are able to

- handle the media

- communicate with employees, and
- advise senior business leaders.

It adds a level of clarity, understanding, and accountability to each individual communicator's role when he or she not only has to think about the press release, but also the internal implications of releasing the message to the media. It also makes for a stronger message when all sides are considered. For instance, telling investors you will reach your numbers by significant internal cost cutting will be a good message for the investors but could be devastating to employee morale and productivity if they haven't been prepared either first or simultaneously.

Yes, there are highly specialized functions that not everyone is the best at: your top PR person who builds strong relationships with top tier media, such as the *Wall Street Journal, Washington Post, Financial Times, New York Times*, BBC, NPR, or an executive speech writer (no, not all communicators are true speech writers, and a presentation is not the same as a speech) who has developed, captured, and articulated the voice of the head of the business.

These highly specialized roles are generally at the fore of thought leadership and cross-business thinking anyway. They already think in an integrated way. Their success depends upon their ability to craft the story, use consistent and compelling messages, and be the best at their craft. Their roles can't be done in a vacuum. They are already integrators.

An integrated communications team—either formally or informally—and an integrated communications strategy with messages that resonate across stakeholders, are the best for achieving business results. And that's what it's all about, right? Results—using communications as a strategic business tool to build or move the business and/or leadership to a new level more quickly, more efficiently, and more effectively.

APPENDIX

Strategy Template

Current Situation

This is the statement of the current state of affairs, the environment in which you must communicate and influence. This section should be straightforward, direct, and unvarnished—accurately depicting what the situation is. Bring in external and internal drivers that are affecting your business and decision making. Include desires of the business leaders. To get results, you cannot sugarcoat reality and expect to get different results than anyone has in the past.

Objectives

This should be a concise list—three to five is best. Make sure these are objectives that communications can accomplish—this is not the full business objectives list, only what communications will influence and achieve results.

Stakeholders

Target, target, target. As highlighted in chapter 7, this is about who you are trying to influence (not merely inform). Be as specific as possible—so if it is customer service representatives, don't merely say "all employees." Managers, the board of directors, senior executives, or all finance employees are specific groups, rather than painting everyone with the same broad brushstrokes and expecting to be able to influence or persuade them all the same way.

Messages

What are the three to five main messages you want to get out? Note: this is not a list of talking points. You can have submessages for targeted stakeholders, but there should be between three to five main messages that are consistent. What will best influence and persuade your stakeholders? What will someone remember if they remember nothing else? They will probably only remember one thing, so make it good.

Strategic Approach

This is the brief explanation of your focus and possibly general methods of communicating.

Measurement

How will you know you've succeeded? Setting standards for success in advance is key. This can include perception research, key performance indicators against individual tactics, surveys, focus groups, meeting feedback, anecdotal feedback, executive satisfaction, etc.

Potential Barriers

List all factors that can get in the way. This helps establish the potentially harmful behavior or pitfalls for which to be on the lookout and calls it out in advance so everyone, including the senior executive team, is aware. This should be straightforward and put any and all elephants on the table. Examples of barriers could be executive behavior not matching their words, logistical obstacles, technology barriers such as with the most creative or social media, out-of-date policies (particularly if you are trying something new), executive team not on the same page, changed behavior threatening the positions of middle management, lack of established budget, not enough people or the right team currently on hand to execute against the strategy, and many others.

Tactics

This is the high-level listing of activities or categories of activities you believe will accomplish your objectives in the most direct way possible.

This should be a targeted list based on whatever research you have garnered at the beginning and not an exhaustive list that uses every trick in the communicator's bag. Each of these will more than likely require an implementation plan. Target and focus are key.

Budget

Self-explanatory—what will it cost and who will pay. The communicator should act as and be seen as a businessperson that is contributing to moving more quickly toward the objectives of the organization. Sometimes, a budget already exists within the communicator's control. More often, the strategy is what will sell the cost of the communications so the business antes up and creates a budget.

Tactical Implementation Plan

Once the strategy is agreed to, the implementation plan needs to be developed and executed. Categories should include the following:

- Individual tactic/activity
- Person responsible—executive owner as well as the staffer doing the work
- Due date—and any applicable milestone dates
- Comments/status

BIOGRAPHIES

Michelle S. Morris began her career in the political world at the White House, worked on presidential and statewide campaigns, was a candidate herself, and then moved to the private sector. She has more than twenty-five years' experience across all areas of communications in a wide range of industries, including chemical, financial services, health care, insurance, technology, pharmaceutical, energy, and maritime. Her specialty is leadership communications—the strategy; messaging; storytelling; executive writing, speech writing, coaching, and counsel; issues management; and creative initiatives that get people's attention, capture their imaginations, and help them align themselves inside the company (employee engagement) and out. Her focus is on communications as a strategic business tool to persuade and motivate people to align with the long-term objectives of the business. Michelle consults with executives at large, medium, and small companies to help them build and get where they wish to go faster and more effectively. She lives in southeastern Connecticut with her family.

Torin M. Lee has had several incarnations within her more-than-fifteen-year career, including campaign field worker, health educator, public relations officer, and employee engagement consultant. Both inside and outside corporate walls, her main focus has been to find creative solutions to make a difference to her target stakeholders as well as the people for whom she works. With a self-professed short attention span, Torin understands the modern worker, what they are interested in, and how they want to get their information—all within the context of a fast-paced world of sound bites that compete for attention in and out of the workplace. Her execution of compelling initiatives that persuade and influence is highly targeted and focused. She enjoys motivating frontline employees and proving how the power of the people really can and does work in any environment. Torin lives in eastern Connecticut with her husband.

www.ingramcontent.com/pod-product-compliance
Lightning Source LLC
Chambersburg PA
CBHW061224280526
45784CB00006B/2627